P...

Trivia
Quiz
Book

William C. MacKay

BARNES
&NOBLE
BOOKS
NEW YORK

The author wishes to thank all who made the writing and production of this book such a delightful task. Among those who provided questions, expertise, or encouragement were Alison Ray, Carol Kelly-Gangi, Sharon Bosley, Robin Hoy, and Hilary Pease. Rick Campbell, Stuart Miller, and Sui Mon Wu sharpened the text in dozens of significant ways. Graphic designer T. R. Lundquist was always interactive and patient.

2000 Barnes & Noble Books

Book design by Lundquist Design, New York

ISBN 0-7607-2103-3

Printed and bound in the United States of America

00 01 02 03 MP 9 8 7 6 5 4 3 2 1

Q: As of July 4, 2000, only four presidents
    were vice presidents when elected. Can
    you name them?

Q: How many presidents were sons of
    presidents?

Q: One president was another president's
    grandfather. Identify them both.

A: John Adams, Thomas Jefferson, Martin Van Buren, and George Bush.

A: One. John Quincy Adams, our sixth president, was the son of John Adams, our second president.

A: William Henry Harrison, our ninth president, was the grandfather of Benjamin Harrison, our twenty-third president.

Q: Who was the shortest American
    president?

Q: Who was the tallest American
    president?

Q: Which president grew up as an orphan?

A: James Madison stood only 5'4". He was probably the lightest American president in history, too: He weighed in at only a hundred pounds.

A: Easy. Abraham Lincoln was 6'4".

A: By the time he was nine, future president Herbert Hoover had lost both parents.

Q: Who was the first president born as an American citizen?

Q: For one president, English was not his mother tongue. Name the president and his first language.

Q: Who popularized the expression "O.K."?

A: Martin Van Buren was the first chief executive born in this country after the Declaration of Independence. All previous American presidents had been born as British subjects.

A: Martin Van Buren grew up speaking Dutch, the first language of his parents.

A: There are several theories about the origin of the expression "o.k.", but one thing is certain, supporters of Martin Van Buren called their favorite candidate "O.K.", for "Old Kinderhook." Van Buren's nickname derived from Kinderhook, New York, his place of birth.

Q: Which presidents were second cousins?

Q: What was the relationship of Theodore Roosevelt and Franklin Delano Roosevelt?

Q: Which President Roosevelt was once Assistant Secretary to the Navy?

Q: Which president said, "The only thing we have to fear is fear itself."

A: James Madison and Zachary Taylor.

A: Franklin Delano Roosevelt was a fifth
cousin of Theodore Roosevelt. F.D.R.
married Theodore Roosevelt's niece,
Eleanor Roosevelt, who was also his own
fifth cousin, once removed.

A: Both. Theodore Roosevelt, in 1897, and
Franklin Delano Roosevelt, in 1913.

A: Franklin Delano Roosevelt, who spoke
the words in his first inaugural speech.
The entire sentence reads: *"So first of all
let me assert my firm belief that the only
thing we have to fear is fear itself—
nameless, unreasoning, unjustified terror
which paralyzes needed efforts to convert
retreat into advance."*

Q: Which American president is credited with introducing macaroni to the United States?

Q: "Macaroni" was also the name of a presidential pet. Who gave this pet to whom?

Q: Which president kept a raccoon named Rebecca?

Q: Which presidential canine attended the signing of the Atlantic Charter?

A: When Jefferson returned from France, where he had served as U.S. Ambassador, he brought with him the first macaroni machine.

A: Vice President Lyndon Johnson gave Macaroni the pony to "first daughter" Caroline Kennedy. Macaroni was one of the first White House pets to receive thousands of letters.

A: Calvin Coolidge. Every day, taciturn Cal visited Rebecca and walked her around the White House on a leash. While the White House was being repaired, Coolidge sent a limousine to retrieve his favorite pet.

A: With his owner, Franklin Delano Roosevelt, and British Prime Minister Winston Churchill, little black Scottish terrier Fala attended the signing of the Charter onboard the U.S.S. Augusta in the mid-Atlantic. Today, a statue of Fala sits not far from his "statue-master" at the Franklin Delano Roosevelt Memorial in Washington, D.C.

Q: What campaign gift did future president Richard Nixon refuse to return in the famous 1952 "Checkers" speech?

Q: Which president threatened a *Washington Post* music critic?

Q: Which future American president served as the president of a union?

Q: When Ronald Reagan left office, he ended what streak?

A: In a televised speech that gained him
     national support, then Republican vice
     presidential candidate Senator Richard
     Nixon told the camera that he would never
     give back his daughters' little cocker spaniel,
     Checkers, to his political contributors. He
     kept his word.

A: Harry S. Truman responded to a hostile
     review of his daughter Margaret's
     Constitution Hall piano concert with a
     handwritten letter to the reviewer Paul
     Hume, which suggested that if they ever met,
     Hume would henceforth need "a new nose
     and a supporter below."

A: From 1947 to 1952 and then from 1959 to
     1960, Ronald Reagan was president of the
     Screen Actors' Guild.

A: At his retirement in 1989, Reagan became
     the first president since James Monroe who
     had been elected in a "zero year" (e.g., 1820,
     1840, 1860) and had not died in office. Seven
     presidents were "victims" of this hex.

Q: Why was the White House painted
white?

Q: Who was the first president to live in the
White House?

Q: When was indoor plumbing installed in
the White House?

Q: What White House fixture had to be
replaced during William Howard Taft's
term?

A: The president's house was painted white to cover the scorch marks left by its burning in 1814 by British troops.

A: The question has two possible answers: John Adams lived in the White House when it was still called The Executive Mansion or the President's House. However, it was James Monroe who presided over the repainting and nicknaming of the White House.

A: During the administration of Millard Fillmore, at Mrs. Fillmore's insistence.

A: A new and larger bathtub was installed after the 332-pound Taft became hopelessly stuck while taking an executive bath. It is said that it took six men to extricate the embarrassed Commander in Chief.

Q: What did the "S" in "Harry S. Truman" stand for?

Q: What was the real full name of Ulysses S. Grant?

Q: Who was Leslie Lynch King, Jr.?

Q: What was Bill Clinton's given birth name?

A: Absolutely nothing. It was purely ornamental.

A: Hiram Ulysses Grant. Grant disliked the initials of his birth name and happily adopted the name a congressman had erroneously given him.

A: The birth name of Gerald R. Ford Jr. His mother took Gerald Rudolf Ford as her second husband shortly before the future president's second birthday.

A: William Jefferson Blythe IV. Clinton's natural father died in an automobile accident before his son's birth. Four years later, Virginia Cassidy Blythe married Roger Clinton, who adopted the future president and gave him his last name.

Q: Which president's pre-White House experience included the hanging of two men?

Q: Which New York City Police Commissioner later became president?

Q: Which sitting American president was arrested?

A: As Sheriff of Erie County, New York, Grover Cleveland personally executed two miscreants.

A: Theodore Roosevelt.

A: President Ulysses S. Grant was arrested for driving his horse-drawn carriage too fast. He was fined twenty dollars.

Q: Who was the last president born in a log cabin?

Q: Who was the first president born in a hospital?

Q: Who was the first president born west of the Mississippi River?

Q: Which president was the son of two immigrants?

A: James Garfield, who was born in Orange, Ohio in 1831.

A: Jimmy Carter, who was born at the Wise Hospital in Plains, Georgia in October 1924.

A: Herbert Hoover was born in West Branch, Iowa in 1874.

A: Andrew Jackson was the son of two Scotch-Irish immigrants who arrived in the United States from County Antrim, Ireland in 1765.

Q: Only one president never had any formal schooling. Who was he?

Q: Who was expelled from college after only one year?

Q: According to literary lore, playwright Eugene O'Neill smashed the window of which future American president?

A: Andrew Johnson. While indentured to a
     tailor, he taught himself to read at night.

A: James Buchanan. After his expulsion
     during his freshman year at Dickinson
     College, he convinced college officials to
     accept him back.

A: Supposedly, O'Neill was expelled from
     Princeton University for breaking glass at
     the house of college president Woodrow
     Wilson. O'Neill attended Princeton
     during Wilson's tenure and committed
     acts of college vandalism which won him
     a suspension. However, the author of *The
     Iceman Cometh* always denied that he had
     ever damaged any of the scholar-
     president's property.

Q: Did any presidents serve in both World
Wars?

Q: How many presidents were participants
in both the Revolutionary War and the
War of 1812?

Q: Which future presidents served in the
Civil War?

A: Only Dwight Eisenhower holds that
    distinction.

A: Only one. Andrew Jackson.

A: Ulysses S. Grant, Rutherford B. Hayes,
    James A. Garfield, Chester Arthur,
    Benjamin Harrison, and William
    McKinley all served in the U.S. Army.
    As Military Governor of Tennessee,
    Andrew Johnson held the rank of
    brigadier-general, but he never thought
    of himself as a military man.

Q: Who is the only person to serve as both President and Chief Justice of the Supreme Court?

Q: Which ex-president served as a congressman in the House of Representatives?

Q: Who was the only president who had also been Speaker of the House of Representatives?

Q: Which president served in the U.S. Senate after being president?

A: William Howard Taft served as
     President (1909-1913) and Chief Justice
     (1921-1930).

A: The year after he left the presidency,
     John Quincy Adams returned to
     Washington as a congressman from
     Massachusetts. He much preferred his
     new job to his old one.

A: Eleventh president James K. Polk.

A: Andrew Johnson, president from 1865 to
     1869, was elected to the U.S. Senate
     from Tennessee in 1875.

Q: Which president served non-consecutive terms?

Q: How many presidents have been elected to three terms?

Q: Who was the only president to serve without being elected as either vice president or president?

A: Grover Cleveland was elected in 1884 and 1892, but was beaten by Benjamin Harrison in 1888.

A: Only one. Franklin Delano Roosevelt won a third term in 1940—and a fourth term in 1944. With the adoption of the Twenty-Second Amendment in 1951, it became unconstitutional for any person to be elected more than twice.

A: Gerald Ford, who became vice president in 1973 after Spiro Agnew resigned; and president in 1974 when Richard Nixon resigned.

Q: Who was the first president to throw out a ceremonial "first pitch" at a major league baseball opener?

Q: Who was the first president to take up golf?

Q: Who was the first ex-president to make a hole-in-one?

Q: Which sports activity did Presidents Ford, Carter, Bush, and Clinton all pursue?

A: William Howard Taft's throw opened
     the 1910 season at Washington's League
     Park. Senator pitcher Walter Johnson
     responded to the presidential presence by
     tossing a one-hit shutout against the
     Athletics. Unlike most later chief
     executives, Taft stayed for the entire
     game.

A: William Howard Taft, who, despite some
     religious protests, inspired an American
     golf boom with his enthusiastic play.

A: Just seven years out of the White House,
     Dwight D. Eisenhower accomplished
     that golfing feat on February 6, 1968 at
     the Lake Country Club, Palm Springs,
     California. As Chief Executive,
     Eisenhower had been sometimes
     criticized for his absorption in the game.

A: Jogging.

Q: Which future presidents graduated from West Point?

Q: Which future president graduated from Annapolis?

Q: One American president was a prisoner of war. Name him and the war.

A: Ulysses S. Grant, class of 1843, and
     Dwight David Eisenhower, class of
     1915, both earned diplomas from the
     U.S. Military Academy.

A: Jimmy Carter graduated from the United
     States Naval Academy in 1946.

A: Andrew Jackson in the Revolutionary
     War.

Q: What historic event occurred at the White House on June 2, 1886?

Q: Which presidents were married twice?

Q: Who was the "Bachelor President"?

A: That day, for the first and only time, a
    U.S. President was married in the White
    House: Grover Cleveland exchanged
    vows with Frances Folsom in the Blue
    Room.

A: James Tyler, Millard Fillmore, Benjamin
    Harrison, Theodore Roosevelt,
    Woodrow Wilson, and Ronald Reagan
    were all twice-married. Widower
    Roosevelt and divorcee Reagan
    remarried before they arrived at the
    White House. Tyler and Wilson both
    remarried while they were president.

A: James Buchanan. Alone among
    American presidents, he never wed.

Q: Which future president won a Pulitzer Prize for biography?

Q: Who was the first American recipient of a Nobel Peace Prize?

Q: Only two presidents have won the Nobel Prize. Who is the second?

A: John F. Kennedy spent his time
     convalescing from a spinal operation by
     writing *Profiles in Courage*. In May 1957,
     this collective biography was awarded the
     Pulitzer.

A: Theodore Roosevelt was awarded the
     1906 prize for his negotiating skills in
     concluding a treaty between Russia and
     Japan to end the Russo-Japanese War.

A: In addition to Theodore Roosevelt, the
     only American chief executive to gain the
     coveted award was Woodrow Wilson,
     who won the 1919 prize.

Q: When were electric lights added to the White House?

Q: Who made the first presidential phone call?

Q: Who had a bowling alley built in the White House?

Q: Who was the first president to have a radio?

Q: Who was the first president to ride in an airplane?

A: In 1891, during Benjamin Harrison's
     administration.

A: Rutherford B. Hayes had a telephone
     installed in the White House in 1879.
     Unfortunately, only the Treasury
     Department also had a phone.

A: The thirty-seventh president, Richard
     M. Nixon.

A: The twenty-ninth president, Warren G.
     Harding.

A: Theodore Roosevelt, who flew in a
     Wright Brothers plane on October 11,
     1910.

Q: Who was the youngest man to become
president?

Q: Who was the youngest man to be elected
president?

Q: Who was the oldest sitting president?

A: Theodore Roosevelt was 42 when he
       assumed the presidency after McKinley's
       assassination in 1901.

A: John F. Kennedy was only 43 when he
       was elected president in 1960.

A: When he left office in 1989, Ronald
       Reagan was 77 years old.

Q: Only one president was elected unanimously. Who was he?

Q: Only three candidates won at least 520 electoral votes in their race for the White House. Who are they?

Q: Five presidents in our history were never elected president. Which presidents achieved the presidency only by succession?

A: George Washington was elected without
      opposition for both of his terms.

A: Franklin Delano Roosevelt garnered 523
      in 1936; Richard Nixon, 520 in 1972;
      and Ronald Reagan, 525 in 1984. Each
      of them was running for a second term.

A: John Tyler, Millard Fillmore, Andrew
      Johnson, Chester Arthur, and Gerald
      Ford.

Q: The following list includes the six presidents with the highest share of the popular vote in an election and the six presidents elected with the lowest share of that vote. Can you extract both lists?

John Quincy Adams	Bill Clinton
Dwight D. Eisenhower	U. S. Grant
Warren G. Harding	Herbert Hoover
Andrew Jackson	Lyndon B. Johnson
John F. Kennedy	Abraham Lincoln
William McKinley	Richard Nixon
Franklin D. Roosevelt	Ronald Reagan
Woodrow Wilson	

A: Only Richard Nixon makes both lists. The six presidents with the highest percentage of the popular vote were: Lyndon B. Johnson in 1964 (61.4%), Richard Nixon in 1972 (60.7%), Warren G. Harding in 1920 (60.5%), Franklin D. Roosevelt in 1936 (60.2%, Ronald Reagan in 1984 (58.8%), and Herbert Hoover in 1928 (58%).

The six presidents elected with the lowest share of the popular vote were: John Quincy Adams in 1824 (30.9%), Abraham Lincoln in 1860 (39.8%), Woodrow Wilson in 1912 (41.8%), Bill Clinton in 1992 (43.2%), Richard Nixon in 1968 (43.4%), and William McKinley in 1900 (43.4%). Adams received fewer popular votes than Andrew Jackson, but was elected by the House of Representatives.

Q: Name the four Chief Executives who won the White House after being defeated as presidential candidates.

Q: All except one of the following presidents was defeated when he was seeking re-election. Name that president.

John Adams	Grover Cleveland
William McKinley	John Quincy Adams
William Howard Taft	George Bush
Benjamin Harrison	Martin Van Buren
Jimmy Carter	Herbert Hoover

A: Thomas Jefferson, Andrew Jackson,
     William Henry Harrison, and Richard
     Nixon. Sixteen years before Franklin
     Delano Roosevelt became president in
     1936, he had been defeated as a vice
     presidential candidate.

A.: William McKinley was elected in both
     1896 and 1900. Unfortunately for him,
     he was assassinated in 1901.

Q: Nathaniel Hawthorne and Henry Wadsworth Longfellow went to college with what future American president?

Q: Only one president was a Rhodes Scholar. Name him.

Q: Which president studied nuclear physics?

Q: Which future president married his teacher?

A: Novelist Hawthorne and poet Longfellow attended Bowdoin College with Franklin Pierce. In fact, Hawthorne wrote his friend Pierce's campaign biography.

A: William Jefferson Clinton.

A: Jimmy Carter.

A: Abigail Powers married her former star pupil Millard Fillmore in 1826. Ever the educator, the first Mrs. Fillmore established the first permanent library in the White House.

Q: Match the nickname with the president:

1. Old Rough & Ready	a. Andrew Jackson
2. Tricky Dicky	b. Martin Van Buren
3. Old Hickory	c. Richard Nixon
4. Tippecanoe	d. Zachary Taylor
5. The Little Magician	e. Jimmy Carter
6. The Man from Plains	f. William Henry Harrison

Q: Who saved scores of lives while working as a lifeguard?

Q: Which president was nicknamed Landslide Lyndon and why?

A: 1. d. Zachary Taylor
    2. c. Richard Nixon
    3. a. Andrew Jackson
    4. f. William Henry Harrison
    5. b. Martin Van Buren
    6. e. Jimmy Carter

A: As a summer lifeguard, college student
    Ronald Reagan rescued more than
    seventy-five people.

A: After Lyndon Johnson won the 1948
    Texas Democratic primary by just 87
    votes out of 988,295 cast, his enemies
    gave him that derisive moniker.

Q: Five presidents were bearded. Who were they?

Q: Bill Clinton, George Bush, Herbert Hoover, Ronald Reagan, James Garfield, and Gerald Ford share one thing in common. What is that attribute?

Q: Which President could write Latin with one hand and Greek with the other?

A: Abraham Lincoln, Ulysses S. Grant,
      James Garfield, Rutherford B. Hayes,
      and Benjamin Harrison all had beards
      while in office.

A: They all wrote left-handed.

A: James A. Garfield.

Q: Which future president was wounded four times during the Civil War and was once listed as dead?

Q: What happened to former President Hayes when he was returning home from President Garfield's inauguration?

A: While serving in the Union Army, Rutherford B. Hayes was hit four times by shells and musket balls. At the battle of Cedar Creek, Virginia in September of 1864, he was wounded; had his horse shot out from under him; and was erroneously reported dead.

A: His train collided with another passenger train. Two people were killed and over twenty injured, but the battle-tested Hayes was only slightly shaken up.

Q: What were the two aspects of William Henry Harrison's inaugural address that made it historic?

Q: Who was the first president to ride to his inauguration in an automobile?

A: First, it was the longest presidential inaugural address in American history, one hour and forty minutes. Second, it probably killed him. Although he was sixty-eight years old and noticeably frail, Harrison insisted on delivering his lengthy address without hat, gloves, or overcoat. The combination of the brisk March weather and a subsequent downpour took its toll. Harrison became ill and never recovered. He died exactly a month after his inaugural.

A: Warren Harding was driven to his 1921 inaugural in a quite horseless buggy.

Q: Who was the first Chief Executive to visit Moscow on an official visit?

Q: Who was the first president to travel to China while in office?

Q: Who was the first president to visit Canada?

A: Richard M. Nixon in 1972. Nixon had
     also visited the U.S.S.R. on government
     business while serving as vice president
     under Dwight D. Eisenhower.

A: Nixon, again, in 1972.

A: Warren G. Harding, who stopped in
     Vancouver on his way to Alaska.

Q: Who was the first president to take office who had been born in the twentieth century?

Q: Who was the last American president to die in the eighteenth century?

Q: How many presidents entered office as widowers?

Q: How many presidents were divorced?

A: John F. Kennedy, born in 1917, took
     office in 1961.

A: George Washington succumbed on
     December 14, 1799, just a few weeks
     before the eighteenth century ended. No
     other president died during that period.

A: Four. Martin Van Buren, Chester A.
     Arthur, Andrew Jackson, and Thomas
     Jefferson.

A: One. Ronald Reagan and actress Jane
     Wyman divorced in 1949. She later
     became one of the stars of TV's *Falcon
     Crest*.

Q: Who was the first president to appear on television?

Q: Who was the first candidate to campaign by telephone?

Q: When were the first presidential candidate debates?

Q: Who was the first candidate to run a front porch campaign?

A: President Franklin Delano Roosevelt
      spoke in televised opening day
      ceremonies at the New York World's Fair
      on April 30, 1939.

A: In 1896, William McKinley kept in
      touch with his campaign managers
      around the country from his home in
      Canton, Ohio.

A: In September and October of 1960,
      Senator John F. Kennedy and Vice
      President Richard Nixon debated four
      times.

A: In 1880, James A. Garfield became the
      first presidential candidate to run his
      campaign from his own home. That
      summer, a telegraph office was set up on
      Garfield's property in Mentor, Ohio, and
      the former General ran his campaign
      without touring extensively.

Q: Which ex-Indian fighter earned a reputation for his prowess as a White House tobacco spitter?

Q: Who had the campaign slogan "Tippecanoe and Tyler Too"?

Q: Identify the president who confided to his successor, *"If you are as happy, my dear sir, on entering this house as I am in leaving it and returning home, [then] you are the happiest man in this country!"*

Q: Which president joined the Confederacy after he was no longer in office?

A: Zachary Taylor, who had spent almost forty years in the army, found himself forced to adjust to Washington manners. His tobacco-chewing skills probably surprised some diplomatic visitors.

A: Ninth President William Henry Harrison, who led troops to military victory over Shawnee Chief Tecumseh at The Battle of Tippecanoe in 1811. John Tyler was his after-thought running mate.

A: James Buchanan. The fifteenth president was so thoroughly disheartened by the Secession Crisis that he expressed his relief to the newly elected president, Abraham Lincoln.

A: Virginian John Tyler was elected as a delegate to the Congress of the Confederacy in 1861 but died before he could take his seat. This rebellious deed won him an unprecedented silence: His death, unlike those of all his predecessors, was not announced by the White House.

Q: Who had the campaign slogan "Happy Days Are Here Again"?

Q: Who had the campaign slogan "I like Ike"?

Q: Which president said, "The chief business of America is business."

Q: Which president had a sign on his desk that asserted "the buck stops here"?

A: Franklin Delano Roosevelt.

A: Ike was the nickname for Dwight
     Eisenhower, our thirty-fourth president.

A: Calvin Coolidge.

A: Harry S. Truman.

Q: Four American presidents have been assassinated. Can you name them and the cities in which they were killed?

Q: Two American presidents were born on the same street in the same city. Can you name them?

Q: Which two presidents are buried in Richmond, Virginia?

A: Both James Garfield and Abraham Lincoln were assassinated in Washington, D.C; John F. Kennedy, of course, was shot in Dallas; and William McKinley was shot in Buffalo, New York.

A: John Adams and John Quincy Adams both arrived in the world on Franklin Street in Braintree (now Quincy), Massachusetts.

A: Virginia-born James Monroe and John Tyler are both buried in Richmond.

Q: How many presidents were members of the Whig Party?

Q: Who was called His Accidency and why?

Q: Name the president who had to endure the insulting chant, "*Ma, Ma, where's my Pa?/ Gone to the White House, ha, ha, ha!*"

A: Four: William Henry Harrison, John Tyler, Zachary Taylor, and Millard Fillmore.

A: When John Tyler succeeded to the presidency after the death of just-inaugurated William Henry Harrison in 1841, his critics said that except for happenstance, he was too mediocre to have acquired the post. Some even argued that the Constitution did not specify that a vice president would become president in the event of the latter's demise.

A: During the raucous presidential campaign of 1884, Grover Cleveland's political enemies discovered that eleven years before, he had fathered an illegitimate son. Cleveland never denied the accusation, but he was elected anyway.

Q: Did George Washington cut down a
cherry tree?

Q: Did George Washington have wooden
teeth?

Q: George Washington is the only
president inaugurated in two cities.
Name the cities.

Q: What was the name of George
Washington's wife?

A: Probably not. Most historians credit
     Parson Mason Loch Weems, an itinerant
     book peddler, with fabricating the tale.

A: Probably not. He had lost his original
     teeth, but, in those days, dentures were
     made of human and animal teeth, ivory
     and lead.

A: On April 30, 1789, Washington was
     sworn in as president in New York City.
     Four years and four days later, he took his
     second oath of office in Philadelphia.

A: Martha Dandridge Custis Washington.

Q: In one way at least, John Tyler was our most productive president. What is his claim to fame?

Q: Two presidents were particularly talented as wrestlers. Can you name them?

A: No other president can match Tyler's fifteen children. (Fourteen of them lived to maturity.)

A: Both Abraham Lincoln and Theodore Roosevelt were known as vigorous, skilled wrestlers.

Q: Which president appointed the first woman to the United States Supreme Court?

Q: Which president appointed the first Jewish associate justice of the Supreme Court?

Q: Who was Joice Heth and why was she famous?

A: In 1981, Ronald Reagan named Sandra Day O'Connor to be a justice.

A: Woodrow Wilson named Louis Brandeis to that post in 1916.

A: Joice Heth was the blind, hymn-singing ex-slave, who had the misfortune of being exhibited by P. T. Barnum as the 161-year-old nurse of George Washington. Not everyone believed Barnum's ruse, but it did help make him a national celebrity.

Q: How many presidents were Roman Catholic?

Q: Who was known as the Preacher President?

Q: Who held the first presidential press conference?

Q: Who held the first "live" news conference?

A: One. John F. Kennedy, 35th President, who was elected in 1960.

A: James A. Garfield, also known as Canal Boy and The Martyr President, was at one time a lay preacher for the Disciples of Christ. Nevertheless, according to a biographer, he had at least one extramarital affair.

A: Woodrow Wilson. Less than two weeks after he took office, Wilson met with over a hundred reporters at the Executive Offices on March 15, 1913. Joseph Patrick Tumulty, the president's private secretary, is generally credited with coming up with the idea.

A: John F. Kennedy on January 25, 1961. Dwight Eisenhower's presidential press conference had appeared on television, but only after it had been edited.

Q: Match the author and the book.

Six Crises	Ronald Reagan
Why England Slept	Gerald Ford
Where's the Rest of Me?	Richard Nixon
Portrait of the Assassin	John F. Kennedy

Q: Which president once lost an entire set
    of White House china in a poker game?

Q: Recite Calvin Coolidge's announcement
    of retirement.

A: Nixon's *Six Crises*; Kennedy's *Why England Slept*; Reagan's *Where's the Rest of Me?* and Gerald Ford's *Portrait of the Assassin*.

A: Warren G. Harding. Harding's love for the game was so strong that his inner circle was known as his "poker cabinet."

A: In entirety, it read: "I do not choose to run for President in 1928."

Q: How many presidents have been impeached?

A: Two, but no presidents have been removed from office by impeachment. Impeachment is the act of formally accusing a public official of crimes or serious misconduct.

Andrew Johnson was impeached by the House of Representatives in 1868, but was acquitted in a trial in the Senate by a single vote.

William J. Clinton was impeached on December 19, 1998 by the House of Representatives, but was acquitted by the Senate by a vote of 55-45 on February 12, 1999.

Richard Nixon was never impeached. The House Committee approved three Articles of Impeachment against him in July 1974, but he announced his resignation on August 8, 1974 before the full House vote.

Q: One president was born on the Fourth of
    July. Which one?

Q: On July 4, 1826, the United States had
    its fiftieth birthday. What else made that
    day memorable?

A: Thirtieth President Calvin Coolidge arrived in the world on July 4, 1872.

A: Former presidents John Adams and Thomas Jefferson both died that day. James Monroe succumbed five years later on Independence Day.

Q: Who was known as The Gentleman
Boss and how did he earn the title?

Q: According to legend, Benjamin
Harrison used profanity only twice in his
life. What caused the future president to
lose control?

Q: Who was called Lemonade Lucy?

A: Chester A. Arthur won this left-handed compliment by running New York City's corrupt customs department with impeccable manners. After Garfield's assassination made him president, Arthur turned on the spoils system that had helped create him, introducing civil service reforms.

A: It is said that once during the Civil War he cursed a Confederate soldier on a battlefield. Years later, he used profanity when he discovered that his father's body had been stolen from its crypt and sold to the Ohio Medical School for dissection.

A: Lucy Webb Hayes, the wife of President Rutherford B. Hayes, earned that nickname for refusing to allow alcohol or wine to be served at the White House during her husband's term. Mrs. Hayes, the first college graduate First Lady, won more friends among prohibitionists than congressmen.

Q: Who served as a congressman, a senator, a vice president, and ran for president against John F. Kennedy?

Q: Match presidents and their prior occupation.

Harry S. Truman	Minister to Russia
Warren G. Harding	mining engineer
Herbert Hoover	newspaper publisher
Jimmy Carter	radio sports announcer
James Buchanan	haberdasher
Ronald Reagan	peanut farmer

A: Two future presidents. Richard M. Nixon
     and, less obviously, Kennedy's
     Democratic Party primary opponent
     Lyndon B. Johnson.

A: Truman/ haberdasher;
     Harding/newspaper publisher;
     Hoover/engineer; Carter/peanut farmer;
     Buchanan/Minister to Russia; and
     Reagan/radio sports announcer.

Q: Two American presidents received gifts of giant cheese. Can you name the Chief Executives and the weight of the cheese?

Q: What All-American delicacy did F.D.R. serve to the King and Queen of England?

Q: Grover Cleveland is famous in candy bar history for what reason?

Q: Which Fresca-loving president installed a soda fountain in the Oval Office?

A: Thomas Jefferson and Andrew Jackson. After Thomas Jefferson was first elected in 1800, a group of Massachusetts supporters sent him "The Mammoth Cheese," a 1500 pound wheel of cheese. In 1835, Andrew Jackson received an almost equally large gift from his enthusiasts, a 1400 pound cheddar cheese which arrived at the White House drawn by twenty-four horses. Shortly before his term expired, Old Hickory invited the public to feast on the cheese. According to legend, it was consumed within two hours. Jefferson's gift never got that far. Already rotting when it reached Washington, it was tossed into the Potomac.

A: Hot dogs.

A: The "Baby Ruth" bar was named for his first daughter Ruth Cleveland.

A: Lyndon Baines Johnson.

Q: What play was Abraham Lincoln
     watching with Mrs. Lincoln when he
     was shot by John Wilkes Booth?

Q: When and where did the play open?

Q: Who was an eyewitness to the Boxer
     Rebellion?

A: *Our American Cousin* at Ford's Theater in Washington, D.C.

A: *Our American Cousin* debuted in Chicago in the summer of 1860. When it opened, the comedy had some major local competition: A few blocks away, at the so-called Wigwam, the Republican Party was meeting to name its first presidential candidate, Abraham Lincoln of Illinois.

A: Herbert Hoover not only witnessed the 1900 Chinese uprising, but the engineer also designed the barricades built to defend westerners in Tientsin.

Q: When was George Washington promoted to the rank of six star General?

Q: Andrew Jackson was Old Hickory. Who was Young Hickory?

Q: Incumbent President George Bush invited lip-readers to parse what message?

Q: Who is buried in Grant's Tomb?

A: President Jimmy Carter posthumously appointed George Washington as the General of the Armies of the United States, specifying that the Father of Our Country would rank first among all generals of the Army, past or present.

A: This was the nickname of James K. Polk.

A: "Read my lips: No new taxes." After Bush signed the tax bill of 1990, his words came back to haunt him.

A: Ulysses S. Grant and his wife, Julia Dent Grant, are buried in the General Grant National Monument, popularly known as Grant's Tomb, in New York City. It is the largest mausoleum in North America.